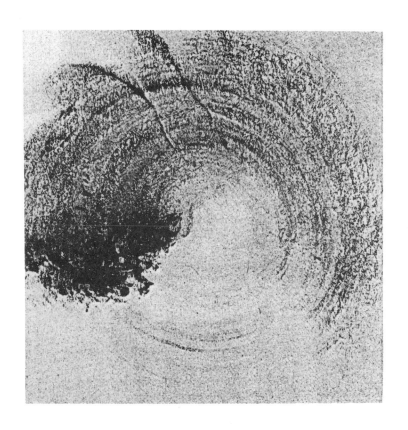

David Michaeli is a teacher of T'ai Chi who is also a writer and painter. In this book, he combines his talents, touching the very essence of T'ai Chi.

DAVID MICHAELI

MOMENTARY REFLECTIONS ON MOVEMENT

Astrolog Publishing House

Astrolog Publishing House
P.O.Box 1123, Hod Hasharon 45111, Israel
TEL/FAX. 972-9-7412044
E-Mail: info@astrolog.co.il
Astrolog Web Site: www.astrolog.co.il

ISBN 965-494-003-5

Published by Astrolog Publishing House 1998

Distribution:
U.S.A & CANADA by APG - associated publishers group
U.K & EUROPE by DEEP BOOKS
EAST ASIA by CKK Ltd

Printed in Israel
10 9 8 7 6 5 4 3 2 1

Contents

Acknowledgements
Nobody creates within empty space.
Everyone is thread spun within a living fabric spread from the
dawn of existence toward infinity.
I am thankful to all the people who were involved in any way in
creating this text.
Special thanks to Nitsan Michaeli for his comments, and to my
family, who are my teachers of love.

Preface

Sensations and encounters
Have come and gone.
Only words remain. Like wave marks on the beach
Like an empty seashell
They are but shells.

Yet, as we stroll along the undulating and ever-changing
Fringe of the sea
It pleases us to see the shell
The squid's bone and the clawprints of the crab.
They remind us that someone was,
and that something still is.

As human beings taking part in this world
We share a common language of metaphors.

Thus something can be sensed among these shells
Scattered across the pages.
Footprints, milestones
And a sense of something familiar.

These pages should be treated
As fragments of poetry.

We cannot live each moment
By written rules or recipes
But we may hear a distant sound.

Introduction

This is an age-old story about the word "knowledge."
Knowledge leads to sensation.
Sensation leads to movement.
Movement leads to understanding.
The memory of understanding is knowledge. The circle is complete.

Stories are told about a person
Who came from beyond the high mountains to a very large country.
When the time came, he surely went the way all humans do,
The way of the entire world.
He completed the circle, so the story tells,
And came to tell us about it.

What we know for certain is that there were groups of people
Who tried to complete the circle.
These people built places to live in.
As individuals and as a group, they did
What all artists have done from the dawn of time:
They sought knowledge and understanding -
The beginning and end of the circle.

These people were guided by the person of whom we spoke
Or perhaps they worked on their own, who knows?
The guidance they received spoke of the next stages of the
process:
They dealt with sensation and movement.
Knowledge was knowledge of the basic assumptions:
Everything flows
Everything has a reason
Don't fight circumstances
Be part of change.

They developed exercises for different sensations.
To feel heat, cold, to look near and far,
Not to look, to feel another's body,
to feel the Earth, to feel the wind,
Not to feel anything - and so on, ad infinitum.

For movement, too, they developed exercises
Combined with sensation so that each faculty would reinforce the
other.
They examined the movement between the body parts,
And the motion of their whole body as one being,
And complete lack of movement,
and movement from the earth to the sky and back through their
bodies.

A more advanced stage of movement and sensation
Was expressed in coordinated movement with others
As tested in the extreme conditions of the martial arts.
From this process emerged an understanding that was stored as
knowledge
That fed sensation, and movement that led to understanding
And so on, round and round.

Knowledge is a seed a kernel.
Dry, hard and small.
Stored in scrolls, books, disks, choreography, words.
It is coded.

The kernel may lie dormant for many years
In proper conditions it grows and blossoms.
Often we hold only fragments of the complete circle.
Thus we accumulate knowledge, but must leave it behind us
In order to experience sensation,
and must leave sensation In order to move.
Finally, we must forget movement
To reach the blossom of understanding.

* If you meet Buddha on the road - kill him.
I focus on the verb "to kill" by mistake,
why and how should we kill?
But we must consider the word "Buddha."
What is Buddha?
The word Buddha in this sentence means understanding,
Now then, we can look upon this sentence with a new light.
If you meet understanding on the road - kill it.
If I refuse to relinquish, if I cling to understanding,
I become imprisoned by rules, and can no longer keep on moving.
But we need not worry.
If we continue along the road
Countless understandings await us.

Student chooses teacher
Through a conscious or unconscious search.
Once found, student faces teacher
In the primeval knowledge of one who is closed
And wishes to be open.
Student faces teacher
Through choosing the possibility to open.
Student faces teacher
So that the teacher may crack open the shell
And create an opening and a door.
This is a frightening process,
Annoying and sometimes horrifying.
The collision may be prolonged.
The shell of fear is fueled
From the student's very core.
And it is this core
That the teacher wishes to reach.
The teacher acts according to his character:
Some attack with full force,
Some give way only to
Return with renewed vigor,
Some are softly seductive.
The right teacher is one with an open gate
Through which the world may pass.
The center that fueled the shell of fear
Is dead.

The student may not communicate with the teacher,
But must stand opposite in order for the teacher
To forge an opening.
Once the door is opened,
Both have the understanding that comes of shared experience
And of loneliness.

Often the guide's gate
Is still not open
And the enormous effort
Invested in opening the student
Actually serves to provide the energy
Needed to open the guide.
Teacher feeds off the student.
The encounter is simple and essentially means:
I want that which seems to you
To be the center of your life.

The right teacher sheds his own shells.
Every so often he leaves his student
For a different kind of encounter
And always he returns a different person,
In a new skin yet ever with the same goal.
This is a form of barter,
The student paying with pieces of himself
For the understandings
And the ability to be a gate.
This is a form of barter in which the student
Must calculate time carefully
In order to build enough of himself
To permit independent and creative life,
In order to build enough of himself
To be capable of severing the connection.

Weight
and Center
of Gravity

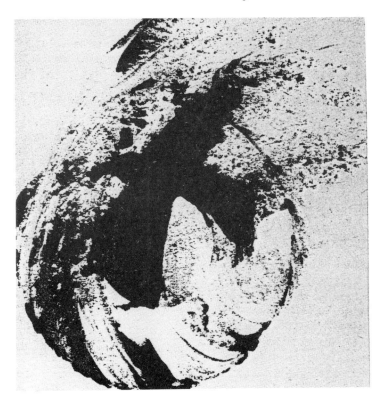

An ancient riddle asks: What color is thunder?
In a similar vein, one might ask: How can we see weight?
Like the wind in a field of wheat
Weight can be seen only through its expression - movement.
Movement exists as the expression of the relationship between objects.
The weight in my hand
Expresses its desire to fall to the ground.
When I release the weight,
It will express itself by moving down toward the ground.
Stopping this movement, as expressed in the effort,
Is weight.
All life forms in the world are expressed in movement.
All life forms in the world are an expression of an unending fall of tension
Toward the center of the Earth,
Which in turn relates to the center of the sun,
Which in turn relates to another center,
And so on, ad infinitum.

Every one of us has a center of gravity.
The center of gravity is an expression of the Earth.
Every thing in the world has a center of gravity.
This center of gravity is a reflection or a miniature model
Of the center of gravity of the Earth.

Every one of us carries the reflection of the Earth within,
Like a chaotic graph on which we detect a loop
Inside of which another loop departs,
With another loop inside,
And so on. We, too, are derivations of derivations
Based on a primordial origin.

When we discover our own private Earth,
Our center of gravity with its sensations,
With all the energy that comes toward us,
We must expose ourselves, we must move our
Shadow back. We must let the shell fall and shine.

At the point of reversal movement, our shadow/body
Swallows the Globe once again
Until the next exposure.

Every joint of our bodies contains the pattern of the Earth.
Every organ has its center of gravity. Every cell and atom.
Thus when energy flows toward us, all the infinite
Centers of gravity are exposed as our shadow/body opens
Like the retreating dark, like a rock emerging from the ebbing
sea.
And when the energy retreats or passes, the shadow covers
again,
The rising water covers the rock, our body swallows up
All this amazing universe.

What color is thunder?
Listen and hear.

Everything that exists on Earth
Has its center of gravity.
The center of gravity is shaped like the planet Earth
And relates to its core.
To discover the personal pattern of the planet Earth
Inside your stomach
Is to see weight independently of form.
Weight expresses the relationship between the center of gravity
And the ground.

The center of gravity is fixed,
Though the form may change.

A person may let his form change along with the surroundings
If he identifies and seizes his inner planet.
Unless he sees his inner planet,
His form cannot change
It will break while changing.

Energy

Energy in movement moves in a straight line.
The straight line becomes a curve
Only when it encounters something stronger than itself.

Any obstacle in the way of energy
Must be attached to the ground,
To the center of planet Earth.

If this obstacle is not properly attached
Energy will uproot it as it continues to move in a straight line.
If it is attached firmly and correctly,
Energy will arch into its curvaceous form.

Energy flies in a straight line.
If we seize it without halting its movement,
And if we are properly attached to the ground,
It will continue to fly, but now around us.

Energy flows in a straight line over a given distance.
It could also flow the same distance in a curve,
Or in twists, or over and over again.
Thus an infinite distance may be traveled
Within an infinitesimal margin of space.

I listen to my fear, I listen to the feeling.
I am connected to my fear, I am connected to the feeling.

If I am pushed, I will fly with the feeling ad infinitum.
With the feeling I can fly in a straight line.
With the feeling I can fly in a twist or curve,
In order to save space and remain within the confines of the
encounter.

A decision must be made to connect to the feeling.
I can use the person who pushes me as an axis
Around which to fly.
(Like a stone tied to a piece of string)
I can create my own axis
And the person pushing me will then become the stone
While I hold the string.

There is no fixed axis or fixed circumference.
They interchange endlessly
Along with the situation.

When the feeling moves beyond the body
And the body remains where it is,
A gulf emerges between the body and the feeling.

When such a gulf exists,
Our sense of equilibrium collapses.
So as not to fall, the body stands firm,
But the fall still occurs, and is expressed in a variety of tensions.

If we wish to maintain our balance, we must strive
To let our bodies move in perfect coordination with our
emotional counterpart
In any direction, without any crack opening up between the two
of us.

If we wish to relate to something in the system moving opposite
us
We should relate only to the gulf.
In this case we must act as gatekeeper
Allowing the feeling to pass and enter
The gulf between it and its body.
In the martial arts encounter,
The system opposite us will disintegrate.

In most cases, the process
Of movement with feeling takes place only partially.
Only the head or torso or lower half of the body
Moves.

We must draw them all together and move with the feeling.

You and yourself - two shadows
Can and must blend into one.
In movement, one of them runs forward
Or backward.
An expression of surfeit emotion.
All that remains is to slide into
The space between this image and its twin.
In proper movement
There will not even be a crack
Between the two images
And it will be impossible to enter between them.

Any energy that moves toward us
Fills us and charges us.
The greater the amount of energy
The more we will be charged
And the heavier we will be.

If our structure is stable and correct
We will be able to bear the continual charge
Without leaking.

We can bear the surplus energy
Charged within us
By directing it toward the mass
To which we relate as part of the fall of cosmic energy.
We can direct the energy
Through the ground
And into the emitting source
Creating a circle.

Energy always works
Symmetrically in both directions.
Energy directed into a crystalline system (such as ourselves)
Will always rebound and echo.

If I stamp my feet on the ground
Or direct weight to the Earth
This will return to me through my soles and joints.

We must relate to ourselves as crystals,
As a ceaseless flow of spinning tops.

Energy does not wait.
When its front point is blocked
It erupts to the sides
Like growths
Like snowflakes
Until it is completed,
Until material is completed
And shaped

When the way is blocked
The river overflows its banks

Movement has its own existence
Any encounter between two masses, objects, materials or people
Creates a single system of movement.

Movement can be seen as the flow between two banks.
The banks may be two hands, two bodies
Or any other type of structure,
Like pizza dough tossed back and forth between the baker's
hands.

Ground

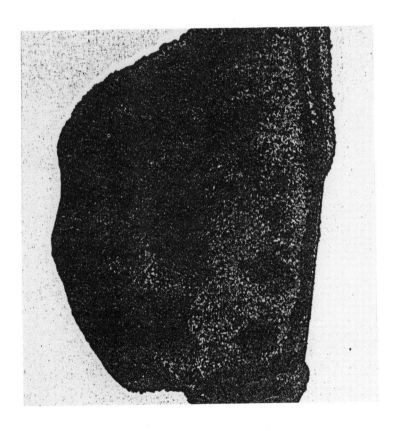

The ground is a full partner in movement.
The ground and myself form a balanced system.
Whenever I define a goal I fall toward it.

Seize the goal and the body is seized.
Seize the ground and the body will be released.

Think of the treading foot,
Not of the outstretched foot.

The ground is the base and the reason for all movement.
Movement is a continuum of states of relationship
Between two objects.
Just as a line is composed of infinite points.
If a single point is missing, the line is broken.

My body opposite the ground
One leg opposite the other
One hand opposite the other leg
My right side opposite my left
One shoulder opposite the other
My head opposite my collar bone
And so on, ad infinitum.

The pattern of an object relative to the ground
Repeats itself endlessly on a large scale and in miniature.
On a large scale:
Myself opposite the ground
The planet opposite the sun.
In miniature:
Particle opposite particle.
And all the possibilities between large and small.

A king may make gestures.
A king has a kingdom —
His stance.
The kingdom is recreated with each step.
You cannot accumulate kingdoms.
When you have a kingdom
You become king.
Make a gesture.

The four directions create the four main winds, and the four additional directions derived therefrom create the secondary winds, and so on.

The encounter of these lines defines a point that would not exist without them. It defines the junction, the point of meeting, the central equilibrium.

As we stand in space, our very existence as an object defines the direction of the weathervane. Like a stone dropped into water.

Thus we stand in the middle of all possible directions. We must observe: a look to the right, a look to the left, a look behind us and a look ahead. We do not fall into the direction defined by our gaze, but we direct our gaze from us to that direction.

We send our thoughts after our gaze, we send our movement after our thoughts. They all come from within us when we are in the center.

When we reach out our hand
There is no reason to fall over.
Every day we finish eating
And push the plate away.
Every day we reach out our hand
To take the fork.
We do not fall over as the plate moves away,
And we do not collapse onto the fork.

Look at your palms
As you would look at flowers
Lift them up like flowers
Bring them toward you
Like flowers
Give them to the person in front of you
Like flowers.

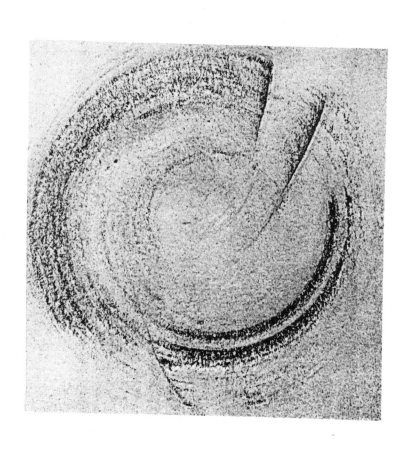

34

Perpendiculr
and Horizontal

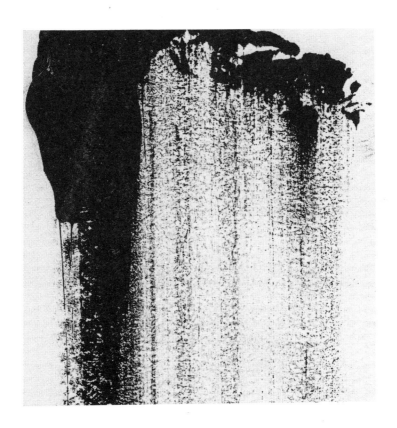

There are three planes of reference
There are three pairs of joints

The shoulder joints create
A plane of reference centered on
The breast-bone.

This is the plane of reference along which
We usually perceive the world.
This is the plane along which
The physical realization of thought will take place
Through the hands, for which the shoulders form the main
joints.

The shoulder joints are able
To move along a lower level
Through powerful connectors - the shoulder blades.

The pair of joints below the shoulders are the thigh joints
Which form a plane of reference
Centered in the lower abdomen
Below the navel.

In order to use this plane
We must think to our knees
Not to our hips.

If use of the thigh joints is faulty or absent,
The connection between the upper plane and the ground
Must pass through another place -
The curve of the spine through the waist, applying
Pressure in a place not intended for this,
As the breast-bone thrusts up and out.

The hands are a tool.
Any tool fascinates us and focuses
Our attention,
Demanding that we realize its use.

Any movement of the hand
Draws attention
To the upper plane, that of the shoulder joints.
The skill is so refined and inherent
That in practice all our communication
With the environment is absorbed and expressed
On this level.

An interesting exercise is to lower our plane of perception (our
attention)
Beneath the waist to the thigh joints
And to raise our hand without our perception rising with it
To the central point of the upper plane.

The channel of movement connecting
All the pairs of joints
Is a perpendicular line flowing from
My head and spine
To the center of the Earth

The other pair of joints is shared between us and the ground.
The encounter between our soles and the ground
Is in its self a joint, and an additional plane of perception.
When our contact with the ground is faulty,
This joint is damaged, and consequently, so are the other joints.

The weight of our body relates
Directly to the center of the Earth.
It constantly seeks to descend to the center of the Earth
In a straight line.
Our adult body resists this movement
With a variety of obstacles.
Each obstacle is eroded by the futile attempt
To block the downward fall or
The relation to the center of the globe.
Through relaxation, we must enable
Weight to flow freely and without interruption,
Just as electricity requires earthing into the ground.

Weight descends like a beam to the point
Of encounter, to the soles.
This beam may be seen as a perpendicular line
Rocked forward or backward,
The beam will scan the foot.
Thus we float across the ground.

* I use my knees and elbows
To carve out and expand the space in which the perpendicular flows.

Slowly it scans from the heel to the cushions of the feet.
If we move back beyond the heel, our body falls -
The beam has moved outside our territory.
We feel the effort in our stomach.
If we move forward beyond the cushions of our feet and on to
our toes
We feel the effort in our back.
Our body falls. We have moved outside our territory.
Our territory is narrow and very short.
But such is the way we live within limited frequency territories:
Temperature, color, odor, sound, etc.
Yet we can perform miracles within these limits.
The horizontal distance is finite
The beam of weight moves with a slight movement.
Instead of stopping at the horizontal border
It turns and dives down
Faced now by an infinite distance.
The movement need not stop. It never stops.
It can gather and overflow, gather and break out,
Or flow in an orderly channel.
We need only create
Its channels.

The encounter between the our feet and the ground
Is the first pair of joints
Creating a lower plane of reference.

The second pair of joints
Are the thigh joints
The third are the shoulder joints.

Movement must flow precisely in this order
Upward like water in a fountain
And must descend in this order
As when the pressure in the fountain is reduced.

The thigh joints and the hip
Serve as a central station
Or as potter's wheel.

When we allow our weight
To fall unhindered to the ground
We are in accord with the fall of tension
Inherent in all things.
Everything we give
Is received back
Immediately, and at an identical pressure.

Our body collects and accumulates the sum of its experiences
In muscular tension of various kinds.
The sum total of tensions and pressures forms
A fingerprint unique to each individual,
The sum of his experience.

If we relate to the sum of all the tensions and pressures in the
body
As matter distinct from ourselves and contained within us,
We will find that this "matter" often
Concentrates on our upper part.

Reactions of fear, astonishment and surprise
Repeatedly draw our attention upward
Until the pattern is frozen
In a fixed form of tensions.

If we try to take this "matter,"
The picture of the tensions,
To melt it and make it flow down into the ground
Our upper part will gradually empty,
And the more empty it becomes the more our spine will be
released.

If we melt this matter but fail to flow down correctly with it
To the ground
The stream of tension will burst out
Perhaps through the waist or the thigh joint.

One of the conditions required in order to melt down our inner
Picture of tensions or statue of tensions
Is to locate the draining point
That is - the hole through which the tension flows.

As in the theory of electricity, we earth
The tension to the ground through the organ
That touches it: the foot.

Filling and emptying necessitates
an exit point to the ground.
Things attached to the ground drain
The pressure vertically,
Like the walls of a building as an external system,
Or like the bones in our internal system.

After we learn
The structure and the exit point
We begin to melt down the picture of tension
Frozen, compressed and fractured,
And we transform it into a constant flow.
Any flow that enters us leaves us
It does not accumulate in our bodies.

When two objects
are born and shaped into this model
(We can acknowledge no other model
Since we are thread spinning into one fabric)
One of them will be the ground
And the other will be the sky,
One is empty and the other full.
One is
And one is not.

Movement will be produced only by exchanging roles.
Empty leg, full leg, left, right, forward, backward.
A system of two objects
One of which refuses to empty or to fill
Means a stuck system.

A body containing a picture of tension so replete
That it cannot exchange the full and empty roles
Behaves as does any blocked system.
Its borders crack, its ability to move decreases
Until it stops.

If two objects which derive their only possible behavior
From the ground, and which contain a replete picture of tension,
Refuse to empty
This will lead to a head-on dispute,
Violence as in any pressured system,
Distress and unbearable pressure, eventually leading to collapse.

I can sit
When the form of the chair exists
And my weight flows to the floor
When the form of the floor exists
And its weight flows into the ground.

As long as the ground exists
And its weight flows into the rock

As long as the rock exists
And its weight flows into change

As long as everything flows
Into the Great Principle.

When I am pushed back
The backward flow will be infinite
But mind will remain still, like a pebble in the stream.
When I am pulled forward
The flow will be infinite
But mind will remain still, like a pebble in the stream.

All material on the Earth
Continually flows in the same direction
Toward the center of gravity.
The flow is spiral, like water in a sink
Like a whirlpool.
Wind, water, earth and crystal
All flow according to the same principle
In the same direction.

This same principle exists in our body.
Every cell and molecule acquiesce to the movement of gravity
And to the fall of tension.
If we manage to direct the movement
Through all the parts in our body, in a fluent and harmonious manner,
By calming and opening these details,
We will receive a smooth flow.
Or else, we will receive an irregular flow
Like water from a faulty faucet
That comes out turbulent and white.

Throughout life, a person gradually accumulates experience
Within his own private picture of tension.
A stage comes when this picture of tension
Begins to melt down and flow.
We call this stage enlightenment.

When we discover the vortex image
Of the center of gravity,
Usually we find it difficult to
Maintain the flow within our body
And to do something else at the same time.

One needs to practice the concept of
Flowing held within
And at the same time to let the
Rest of the body and its movement
Be vivid, light and free.

Let your stomach be relaxed
While your spirit is gathered in.

Matter
and Change

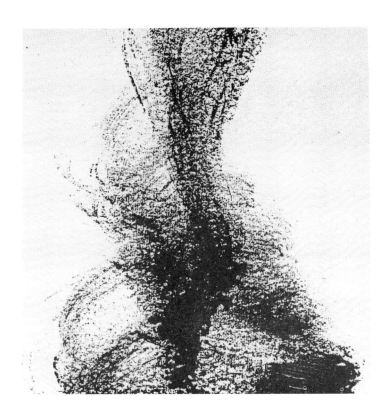

We are composed of a mass of crystals
Which combine to form a fabric.
This fabric may move or remain still
Within another complete tapestry.

We must teach our vision and sense of touch
To discover holes or ridges in the fabric.
Every fabric has the potential for movement.
When the fabric is soft,
Movement flows through it with ease
Like the wind whipping up waves on the water.

Mass must be allowed to move down
In its natural direction.

Mass given to the ground
Is returned at equal pressure.
If the fabric remains open
The wind of the earth may flow up.
The fabric may be left open
Until the earth can blow from the head
Or be expressed from any other point in the fabric.

Afraid to lose our perception of our body
We lose our life.

I am sinking
Sound reverberates along my body
The ground blows through my feet
My head sways in the wind.

The wave softly flows down
To the ground, to the beginning of the world.

The wave softly flows up
To the human, to the end of the world
The wind blows from my hand
My head sways in the wind.

The wave or movement
Does not flow in a linear manner,
But sweep across entire space.

Within the fabric of movement,
frozen spots which do not move
Due to tension, injury, or any
Other obstacle, may be detected.

In terms of movement, anything that does not move is dead.
Thus we must strive to see that every possible point in our bodies
Moves, when we are in motion.

When the potential for movement builds up in your body,
Expend it instead of fighting it.

To resist the movement potential
Is to cling to a template
After a change has occurred.

Every object and every substance
Is the footprint, pattern or documentation
Of directions meeting.

Every object is a fossil,
A memorial to a process
That passed through matter
And left its mark.

Thoughts and sensations about a concept
Are also a memorial to a process
Which once was, and is no more.
A memorial to an occurrence or event
Is called an experience.
The process of life is perpetual motion
A never ending change
In the infinite fall of tension.
We are always capable of moving
With the wave of movement, with the wave of becoming
Without being fixed on a concept, direction or matter,
Without leaving a mark,
Without leaving patterns behind us,
Without leaving memorials behind us,
Without looking back.
Only then will we be able to live.
Anyone who looks back
                    Freezes, fossilizes and dies.

Only if we choose perpetual change
Which in any case happens
May we live.

All our actions leave a mark,
Pattern, record or footprint of some kind.
The footprints of our actions
Are proof and confirmation for us
That we indeed acted
That we are indeed living beings.

Becoming addicted to these footprints
Is to lose the way and the ability
To act and to live.

We must regard the point of contact
Or encounter
As a living, becoming, changing and moving being.

If we become fixated by form
The point of contact has already eluded us
And moved on.

Contact burns.
Encounter is a wound.
Look at it,
Do not look at the form.
Always changing
Always twisting
Always being
Leave its footprints
Forget its result
Seek for the moment when it happens
Then you will not have
Time to breathe.

Things always appear obscure.
The desire to focus,
To behold things clearly and sharply,
Actually causes them to disappear.

Even when something appears very clear and sharp
It is good to blur it a little
For we may then absorb more of its spirit.

Fear prevents me from letting go of things.
I cling on fiercely
Trying to make them clear, sharp, precise.
Without obscure and uncertain margins,
All for my sense of security.

Yet clear things always disintegrate
Leaving me frustrated and disconcerted.
Instead of seeking the form of things
We should seek for the principle.
What is the principle?
The principle is invisible
It cannot be perceived in a conscious manner
Yet it may be understood
In terms of our body or spirit.
We can live with it, live within it,
Yet if we try to seize it, it vanishes.
Therefore, either perception (definition) or existence.

According to this understanding
It is pointless to adopt any thoughts or insights
That were valid the moment at which they occurred,
Even though they enabled us to see things
Correctly.
There is no point deriving a way of life from these thoughts or insights
Since as soon as I adopt them as a scenario
As soon as I touch them
They become fossils
And existence flows on.

Sequence has no meaning.
Order enables us to look forward
To lean, to rest, to sleep.

Order causes us to develop expectations.
Think about the foothold,
Not the outstretched leg.

Weight means value.

Transferring weight means transferring value.
Transferring weight means transferring thoughts and feelings.
Transfer all your values wholly
Transfer all existence completely.

There is a perception
And there is that which you perceive.
These are two separate concepts.
Perception is an instrument.
That which you perceive changes.

When trust is absent
Addiction to rhythm sets in.
Leave your shadow with every step
Leave yourself behind with every new step
And get out.

When someone comes to you
Listen, listen.
What does he want?
What does he want?
Listen.

The tension springs up
To the shoulder joints
And chest
Fossilizes and fixates the shoulder blades.

The fixation of the shoulder blades
Forces us to produce movement
Through curving and bending
The spine in various ways,
None of which is necessary.

The shoulder blades move
Relative to the spine.
The spine moves
Relative to the shoulder blades.
The bones move
In relation to the muscles.

We should regard ourselves
As a gloved hand.
The glove is our body.
The hand is our spirit.
When the hand moves,
The glove moves along with it.

The extremities of our body move
Like the end of a whip.
When movement is flowing
Through the base of the whip,
The wave sweeps to the ends.
The continuous flow of movement back and forth
Feeds the wave
In a curve toward the ends
And ends with the crack of the whip.
The base of the whip is the thighs.

Axis
and Relativity

When I fall to the source
There is an axis.
When there is an axis
There is symmetry.

In touch
Not too much
Not too little
Then we touch
The chords of the world.

The chords of the world
Are connected everywhere
And to every thing
Touch the chord
And the chord will carry you
Anywhere.

People confuse the concepts diffuse and empty
Means something without a framework (without a way)
Empty means naught in a framework (the way)

Disparity has no point of reference
That which is empty relates to the center.

The cup of tea is a reality between ramifications.

When I am in movement I stir the room.
One cannot stir with a broken spoon.

All movements in the world
Exist as the result of a constant fall of tension.
The growth of an infinite number of things
Is the result of the infinite fall.

All movements in the world
Exist as the result of a constant fall of tension.
It accumulates in a sunken area
Until it fills and continues the fall
Beyond its bounds.

I create an expanse
The expanse is a field of time and space.
You and I move over the expanse
I view the expanse from above

I create a field
I look upon the field from above
You run in the field
I am your shadow.

When I cannot see the field anymore
I am no longer your shadow.
Your movement creases the expanse
And uproots me from my place.

I can sense the gravity
Of any object in space
In relation to myself.

Relating to space
Is through the weight of the objects
Which move therein.

By using observation
I create the space
By using the perception
Of other objects, space is created.

I must not make my space rigid
For then the object that moves therein
Will crease and tear both it and me.
I must let space remain fluid.

The world is a garden of gravity flowers
All different objects, all forms,
Are gravity flowers.

Each meeting of vectors creates a point in space.
When the directions relate to each other
,The point is static,
And the relation exists in the flow of movement to that point
Like a bow on a violin string.

When the objects or the directions
Are locked in one another
The point moves with them
And the weakest of them is stretched and torn.

As humans we have the ability to observe.
If we observe the point,
We can move with or without it
But observation means
Our relation to the point.

When we do not see the point
This is a sign that it has passed us
And moved over us to the other side
This is a sign that we did not maintain
A relationship with the point
And are blind to it.

I know now that in any relationship,
However long or short it may be,
There is a moment of potential union.
When this occurs, there is no time, no us, no world.

In Hebrew, the word "victory" comes from the root meaning
"eternity."
The surfer does not vanquish the wave
The man does not vanquish the woman
The killer does not vanquish the killed.

Both are united in a single moment
Both are at the door.
The nature of the encounter will determine — heaven or hell
Both share eternity.

Time,
And the rhythm derived from it,
Are determined solely in relation
To another system
When you are with the system
There is nothing to relate to
There is no time, no distance. The world has stopped.

Life is the movement between two parts.
Life is dissonance.

In the crack between two blocks, life appears
Life is the result of a breakage.

In doubt
A new thing is born.

Life is the expression of the relationship
Between two objects.

A completely symmetrical face
Is lifeless and frozen
Asymmetry between the two sides
Creates movement and character.

In the crack in the rock grass grows
In the crevice in the hill water flows
In the space between two houses people pass.

Thus we do not have to struggle
To create life
But merely to open the space.

There is something there
It is almost tangible,
But cannot be reached.
Yet the knowledge
Gives me happiness
For there it is.

Observation
and Perception

We produce movement from within three fields.
The first field is imitation.
The second field is habit.
The third field is necessity.
If I produce movement
From within a fourth field of will or attention
My body will move
Along the path of attention.

Each of us transmits.
Hunger, fear, satisfaction, pain, calm, etc.
All our sensations and their results
Are continuously transmitted in posture,
In various positions and various manners of movement.

There is only one possibility.
Either to transmit or to receive.
When we transmit, we cannot receive
When we do not transmit, we receive.

In order to be in a state of reception we must stop transmitting.
We stop transmitting by decision
We stop transmitting as the result
Of extreme external intervention.
In a state of reception, the entire body receives
Whatever its movements and purpose of movement may be.
The hand receives to the same extent whether it is moving forward
Or backward.
As we listen to our pulse
As we caress a body
In the state of transmission, we suffer from blindness,
In the state of reception, we can see.

In order to stop transmission
We must relinquish all
Accumulated statements of our body.
Gasses, itching, back pain, knee pain
Visual image heart pain
And whatever one might imagine.

It is impossible for us to force ourselves to stop transmitting.
With experience and practice, it happens by itself.
When transmission stops — reception begins.
When reception begins — we can see.
It does not matter what we see
The main point is that I am not asleep, not blind
I am awake.

Frogs have a system of vision that responds only to movement
When something is not moving, the frog cannot see it.

Our vision is a development of the same principle.
We discern movement, and we discern the potential
For movement reflected in various types of vectors —
Straight and curved — of shapes.
From a number of isolated points we conceive
The complete image of possible movement.

And yet, just like the frog, we still do not discern
The lack of movement.
How can we find lack of movement?
Between two directions or two definitions of movement
There is an area of lack of movement.
We can learn to observe the areas
Between directions
As we discern the pauses between sounds.

Our habitual routine of observation
Prevents us from observing in other ways.
The habitual routine we employ
Leads us to identify the borders and texture
Of an object in a two-dimensional or spatial manner.
Partially.

We automatically divide any object
According to the relation of our body parts.
The manner in which we observe any object
Or any surface is toward the approximate point
At which the eyes are located
In relation to the face.

This division is automatic and infinite
So that as we move down to smaller parts
They will be divided accordingly
And the more we generalize, the division will relate to new
volume.

At the point of focus
(Which is the height of the eyes in relation to the face)
Our spatial perception is at its best
At other points of the object
On which we do not focus
It deteriorates to two-dimensional perception.

Another manner of observation
Is to perceive the object from a different point
Like the difference between a drawing without perspective
And a drawing with perspective.

It is possible to develop a perspective view of the object
And to look at it from underneath.
Like the bottom of a pan.

When you have seen the underneath
You have seen the entire object
In terms of its movement or growth.
In effect, the genealogy of its movement
You have expanded your spatial vision.

The manner and result of observation —
The sensation and conscience,
Determine the way
In which the body carries itself.
Training parts of the body
And practicing movement
Will add nothing
If observation remains unchanged.

Change the manner of observation
And all your body will follow your mind.
Observation determines the pace of movement.
Through this observation you can see any object
In your surroundings from underneath.
The world is a garden of gravity flowers.
When you see any object from its root,
The world radiates.

When we observe a drawing, we habitually see
The lines of which it is composed.
We think: The lines are the drawing.
This is a partial way of seeing things.
The picture is essentially the spaces defined by the lines.
The line cuts the space and shapes its form.
The line delimits space.
In our normal mode of vision
We think that only the line exists.
The space cut
In one way or another
Is what gives us sensation.
Space defined correctly
Is a complete universe.
Space defined incorrectly
Is a broken universe.

In movement, our movements are the pencil or paintbrush,
The movements shape, border and define spaces.
An incorrect movement means broken space, a shattered universe.
A correct movement defines a complete space.
When we are in motion, we must draw and create
Complete and dynamic spaces like the movements of soap bubbles
On changing frames.
Not torn, shining and moving.
When I move with another person or another object
Together we define a common space with which we play.

The hands have two functions:
1. To seize, hold, gather, collect, support.
2. To delimit areas and to define space.

When we observe movement in terms of near and far
Volume diminishes to the point of reversal, where it once again
becomes infinite.
The hand, body or object coming toward me
Closes the space between us
The space between us gradually escapes into the
Surrounding expanse.
When the space is reduced to nothing
I am wholly located in the surrounding area.
Then it is possible to open by pressure
A new inner space
When the space around flows in
From all directions.

It is a mistake to think about the amount of space available to
me
In economic terms
Or to think of how to preserve these amounts of space,
Or how to keep something in my possession.

This is like clinging on to a glass of water with all my might
When I stand in a sea.
We need to throw the glass away.
Any economic line of thought means practices
Designed to preserve the glass.
Since the space around is infinite
And is infinitely available to me
There is no need for economic thought
Which implies the fear of loss
And the desire to keep possessions.

Sensation belongs to the bones.
Rational thought belongs to the flesh.
Sensation is sensation. It cannot be compared to anything.
Rationality means comparison to a data base and deduction.
Any sensation is reflected or expressed immediately in the bone.
The sensation in our bones causes a reaction in the soft tissues of the muscles.
This reaction is registered, processed and stored as a memory,
Ready to be recycled.
The bone is the sensor and the source of sensation, like a seismograph.
But all the soft tissues around the bone
Accept the sensation as a secondary medium
And engage in reaction, in storing information and in comparing it to the current data base.
The comparison to the existing information data base, together with our impulse to collect and to accumulate,
Creates a reaction of unwillingness to release information or to receive information
Incompatible with the existing information data base.
In order to receive new information, we must release existing information.
The usual reaction is hardening the soft tissue,
And blocking the possibility of expression of the bones.
It is worth understanding that our bones receive everything and every change.

When the bone feels
The flesh compares and reacts.

The flesh has food of its own
And the bones have food of their own.

We are gateways
Between one thing and another.
We have the ability to open the gateway
We have the ability to keep it open.
We are the gateway
We are the expediters
The river of existence flows through us.

The flow exists because the river has banks.
The river never ceases.
The direction of the flow is determined by the banks
By the great fall of tension
Like the branches of a tree in different directions.
Although the trunk is vertical, there are horizontal branches
Which relate to it.

The attention
Must unite
With the direction of flow.

The technique is not a tool for collecting anything.
The technique — any technique — is a way
To identify and to hunt my habits and my patterns
And to rid myself of them.
I do so in order to open a gateway
To my center
To the quiet place in the center of the storm
Of my reactions and instincts.
This center is the gateway to the world.

The bones are the residence of sensations.
The flesh stores and is recreated by memory and reaction.
Let your bones move freely within your flesh.
When your flesh hardens, you become stiffened.
Give your flesh wholeheartedly to your partner in meeting.
Release your bone from the grip of your flesh
And then you will understand what the bone says
The voice of the world will be released through the bone.

Be transparent
Give your partner in meeting
The ability to see through you.

Connection
and Structure

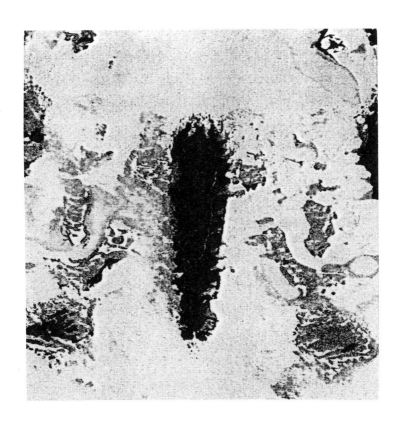

When we meet a rival we must relate to him as we would to our
own body
Which had decided to turn against us.
When my hand is lifted to my face, the hand's conscience is
Also my own. If I do not want it to reach my face, it will not do
so —
Either by means of an inner decision causing the hand to drop,
or by
Means of my other hand, if I wish to play. When both hands
are lifted to my face
The inner decision is obviously sufficient.
Just as no sane person would strike himself, so our conscience
Will encompass our rival and make him part of it, and so his
conscience will
Become my own. His body will be my body, and I must
maintain my inner dance between myself and my/his body.

The meaning of structure is two coordinated things, or two things in a single motion, such as the inter-connected atoms that comprise a molecule.

Understanding has no reward.
Understanding is an object.
Like a stone.
What is the reward for a stone?
What is the reward for water?
What is the reward for air?
Understanding has no reward.
It is only understanding.

All horizontal lines in the universe are bridges. It does not matter whether they are defined as a channel, as a road or as a line in the sky. Like the graphic lines in a model of a molecule, which link atom to atom.

All vertical lines in the universe point to its center. The significance of the connection to the center is an entity, an object. An object may stand by itself. Through meeting another object, it is possible to forge a horizontal connection. Now it will be a system comprising two objects with a horizontal connection. A bridge. A communication line. A tension. A field. It doesn't matter what we call it, this is a hovering connection of horizontal orientation between two or more points relating to the center of the planet, to the center of the universe, in vertical. This is the significance of structure.

When we place our attention or our foot on the bridge, we walk across an abyss. Our whole body stiffens because our behavior patterns assault us, locking us in the four bolts. Alternatively, our behavior pattern may collapse. This is an over-reaction with a paradoxical result, just like the immune system protects the body in which it dwells by attacking it. The only way is to act contrary to reason or to the so-called "common sense" of the locking system and of the ways in which it interprets reality. We must open the four locks in order for the fall of tension to exist in our bodies toward the center of the planet. Then we will cross the tightrope above the arena of uncertainty.

The acrobat who crosses a tightrope maintains a total and complete awareness of the vertical points and directions to the center of the planet. As soon as he fearfully stiffens, he will cut the directions on which he stands, and fall.

Our automatic mode of walking in the street is a highly-skilled and acrobatic act of skipping and falling from one foot to the other. We blindly throw ourselves from foot to foot in a constant state of floating. If we try to leave one leg in the air during a normal movement, we will always fall.

Conscious walking through permanent examination and curiosity will always relate to the ground rather than to a target, and will create an unceasing sequence of vertical and downward contacts, receiving constant feedback from the ground. The ground will in turn flood our bodies from bottom to top. At each such complete point we shall form a solid basis for drawing a horizontal line of connection — a bridge.

The person who draws this line may cut it when his rival / partner is upon it, his rival will then fall.

Our attempts to reach the horizon are the way to the other.
They are the significance of our existence; the reason, the way
and the continuation.
Our attempts to reach up or down are the way to ourselves.
These are two opposite sides of the same coin.
Without touching ourselves, we cannot complete our way to the
other.
And our way to the other entails self-discovery.

I must take my partner in movement as a tugboat pulls boats on the river. I must feel the river in which both he and I stand.

There are four main bolts in our body, which are the expressions of the state of our patterns of behavior and movement.

The pattern of behavior is the reflection of the pattern of movement, because the movement is the implementation of the fight or flight instinct.

The bolts are the main sinews of the two shoulder joints and the two thigh joints. Mostly, except during rest or relaxation, they are in a state of tension or semi-tension, that is to say: locked or half locked. Any movement which threatens to uproot me causes the bolts to lock in order to maintain the status quo. Doing this, however, I lose both the pattern and its content, if the encountered force is too fierce for the pattern to hold, or is directed at the exact point of disassembly. Accordingly, I must perform an action which contradicts my instinct.

I must open the bolts in order to be free and to descend to the root.

When I descend to the root, there appears an alternative to the fight or flight instinct. The alternative is the connection, the bridge, and the ability to move thereupon, together with the other.

We observe objects, but we do not see the connections.
We can see the connections and the bridges
The relations between objects.
Each is a way of observation.
The person who can see the connections
Is perceived as a wizard by the person who can only see the object.
Yet finally it is only a technique.
Forget them both.

Epilogue

You must be irresponsible in order to walk toward the tiny
unknown
Between one footstep and the next.
Unable to free ourselves of fear, we blindly
Throw ourselves with rigid body into the next inevitable step.
The center of gravity, the core of the planet, wishes and deserves
to be born. The pattern of our behavior, which was a highly
valuable support in its time, eventually must come to be
dismantled so as not to prevent this birth.

Afraid to look
Seizing the lintel
By the window.